Cryptocurrency

An Essential Guide To Accomplishing Successful
Navigation Through The Digital Asset Landscape

*(Simplifying Cryptocurrency Investments While Providing
A Useful Guide To Build Your Portfolio)*

Pancrazio Masiero

TABLE OF CONTENT

The Workings And Principles Behind Cryptocurrency

There is no way around the fact that the mechanisms behind cryptocurrencies are extremely complicated. The workings of a cryptocurrency can be difficult to understand, even for early investors and consumers of the technology. In this chapter, we will discuss the inner workings of cryptocurrencies and how they operate. It is better to begin at the beginning and work one's way up, abstracting fundamental concepts into the larger field of bitcoin. Our first order of business is to take a closer examination of a block, the fundamental building element of any blockchain that records transactions for a cryptocurrency. Following an examination of the structure of the block, we will investigate the formation of blocks and the subsequent use of cryptography to link blocks into chains. After that, you should educate yourself on the distributed ledger, which is the underlying network that cryptocurrencies are based on. Mining, which is the process through which new cryptocurrencies are generated and distributed, will also be broken down into its component steps in this section. Following that, further information will be provided on wallets, which are the primary method for storing cryptocurrencies. In the final part of this series, we will discuss the anonymity that cryptocurrencies provide and the process by which cryptocoins are transferred between individuals and institutions.

What's contained within a block? In the field of computer science, "record" refers to the underlying data type, and "block" is an abstraction of "record." A record can be thought of as being analogous to an entry on a table. Each "record" on a blockchain, such as the one that underpins Bitcoin, comprises a number of different "fields." In this table, a field functions similarly to a column. Each field contains a certain kind of data that is intended to fulfill a particular function. One way to think of these recordings is as if they were pages in a book. Every page is connected to the next one using links. Hashes derived from cryptography are used in this instance to bind the pages together. In a nutshell, a block is a record that contains many data fields. When it comes to the blockchain, each record consists of five different fields.

The "magic number," the blocksize, the blockheader, the transaction counter, and the transaction data are the five different forms of data that are contained within Bitcoin blocks. The magic number is a one-of-a-kind identifier number that establishes the block as an integral component of the network. The blocksize parameter stipulates the precise dimensions of the block to be created. The blockheader is a complicated field that is made up of six other fields that are included within it. It is probable that the blockheader is the most crucial component that makes up a block. A number that maintains track of the total number of transactions that have taken place is referred to as the transaction counter. The final piece of the puzzle is the transaction data, which contains the real information on which coins are being moved to which addresses.

Examining the blockheader's six fields is necessary if we are going to have a grasp on what it represents. These are the version, the hash of the block that came before this one, the hash of the block that's being worked on right now, the timestamp, the target, and the nonce number. The version specifies the software version in which the block is currently running. This block is connected to the one before it by the hash of the block that came before it, as was discussed above. The hash of the currently active block is saved in a way quite similar to that immediately after it. The timestamp is a value that maintains track of the date and time that the data was last updated. This value is expressed in seconds. A timestamp that is encrypted provides evidence that the material has not been altered in any way. The goal is a value that specifies how challenging it is to verify the currently active block. Last but not least, the nonce number is a value that clients on the network employ whenever they make an effort to validate the hash.

All of these variables have to be computed by a machine each time a new block is added to the blockchain. All of the values for the fields in the records are imported in the order that is listed by either calculating them or reading them from the block that comes before. The generation of new blocks is the fundamental activity that underpins bitcoin. In order for a cryptocurrency to expand, new blocks need to be generated and added to the blockchain on a consistent basis. The data pertaining to transactions that are taking place on the network makes up the vast majority of the information included in these blocks. As we have seen previously, having a record of all transaction data that is both comprehensive and safe provides a comprehensive picture of who owns which coins and where they are going.

Who is responsible for making these blocks? Because of the decentralized structure of the blockchain network, every user that participates in the transaction of a cryptocurrency has some input towards the creation of blocks. Users on a blockchain network share the computing power necessary to complete the activities involved in adding new blocks to the ledger and connecting existing blocks together. In point of fact, people who are linked to the blockchain constitute the entirety of the network. One of the numerous precautions taken in the realm of cryptocurrencies, the peer-to-peer approach is designed to ensure that there is no centralized authority or middleman that has the ability to manipulate or modify essential transaction details. This is the procedure that enables new blocks to be added to the blockchain of a cryptocurrency.

Putting these blocks in a row and then chaining them together is an essential part of the process of making new blocks. A hash of the preceding block must be included in the blockhead of each new block before it can be considered complete. Any new block that is added must link to the one that came before it in this manner. This procedure makes it possible for any user to view and read transaction data from blocks, but it prohibits any user from illegally tampering with or manipulating the transaction data in any way. The process of linking blocks together in a blockchain generates data that is not only entirely open to public inspection, but also generates data that is practically difficult to corrupt by hacking or manipulation.

Lines of trend

It is not always simple to recognize the trend in the industry. You might be able to tell that the market is in an uptrend if there is a lot of price movement; but, you won't be able to tell how steep the slope is or how quickly prices are climbing if there is a lot of price movement. Because you are taking in all of the noise, it is challenging for you to recognize the signal, which is the actual trend.

You may find it easier to understand the trend if you draw trendlines on the chart. Basically, if the market is in an uptrend, you will aim to locate a line that it keeps coming back to at the bottom. This line will serve as a support level. Locate the places where the price is at its lowest, and then link those points together. You are really fortunate. In contrast, this task required a pencil and a ruler up to the late 1980s, and the software will either do it for you or at least assist you in doing it. You should now have a chart that seems as though all of the peaks are "sitting" on a line of support. This is the result you should have expected.

When dealing with a market that is experiencing a downward trend, you will need to adjust your strategy accordingly. You are going to create a line that passes through the highest highs; these are the points at which the price reaches when it bounces, but it eventually loses momentum and begins to fall again.

Okay, so I started out by presenting you with some hand-drawn illustrations of support and opposition. This time, instead of delaying our entry into the real world, let's go ahead and check out Amazon. I went on StockCharts, and I just couldn't believe what a great example of a channel I'd gotten, so I stuck it into my drawing software and put in the trendlines. The real trendline is the straight one underneath, that's pushing it upwards, but you can also see there's a straight resistance trendline at the top of the chart. (The other two winding lines are moving averages, which will be discussed in more detail later.)

The Very Best Trading Strategies For Cryptocurrencies

In the market for cryptocurrencies, there are specialized instruments that may assist traders in gaining a competitive advantage. INDICATORS is the term that is most generally used to refer to these instruments. When developing mathematical models of how prices have behaved in the past, technical analysis mainly relies on the corresponding historical data. These models are subsequently used as indicators. The information that is taken from the formulae is plotted on a graph, which is then placed adjacent to (or superimposed over) a trading chart. Traders are able to readily express their selections with the help of this image. However, these indicators are not capable of predicting price changes with a precision of one hundred percent.

The following is a list of the most effective and user-friendly technical analysis indicators that are fully compatible with various forms of digital currency, including Bitcoin, Ethereum, Litecoin, Ripple, and EOS. When you have mastered these methods, you will also acquire an advantage in other markets such as stocks, currencies, and commodities. Learning these techniques for risk management and developing your trading abilities is therefore something that is well worth the time and effort that it takes to do so.

The relative strength index, sometimes known as RSI

The RELATIVE STRENGTH INDEX (RSI) is an easy approach, which makes it a constructive trading strategy that may generate profits and frequently results in a favorable conclusion. Welles Wilder, a technical analyst, invented the Relative Strength Index (RSI) almost forty years ago to assist traders in determining when the price of Bitcoin deviated too far from its actual value. Because of this knowledge, the traders are better able to capitalize on opportunities for progress before the market rebalances itself.

The Relative Strength Index (RSI) is a technical indicator that uses a convoluted formula to determine whether or not a cryptocurrency (or another asset) has been overbought or oversold. A number ranging from zero to one hundred is what the formula gives back, and either an oscillator or a graph may be used to illustrate this range on the chart.

RSI Plus 100 Less Than 100 Times One Plus RS

RS equals the average of N periods' closes up minus the average of N periods' closes down N is the number of periods. It is strongly suggested that you use 14, but you are free to use whatever number you wish.

When the Relative Strength Index (RSI) drops below 30, a cryptocurrency or asset may be deemed cheap or oversold.

The Pros and Cons of Repetitive Strain Injury (RSI)

Traders may use the RSI to get insight into existing trends as well as trends that are already beginning to lose strength. It is simple to grasp and straightforward to implement in order to develop a profitable trading strategy, in particular when paired with candlesticks, charts, and several other models.

The Relative Strength Index (RSI) is widely regarded as one of the most reliable trading systems, despite having a large number of potential drawbacks. However, in order to avoid losses, traders should make an effort to increase their sensitivity to situations that are considered to be overbought or oversold.

How Are Individual Blocks Linked Together On A Blockchain?

When a block is completed, a timestamp is used to assign a number to it. In addition to receiving a reward, the miner who discovered the block is entitled to the transaction fees associated with all of the transactions that were included in the block. In the case of Bitcoin, this corresponds to the previously indicated 12.5 bitcoins every block; but, as time passes, this number will gradually decrease. If a transaction is included in this block, then that transaction will be confirmed for the very first time right now. Within a few milliseconds, many thousands or perhaps millions of miners will replicate that block and begin mining on the new block. They will do this by utilizing the last puzzle piece from the most recent block, adding new transaction puzzle parts, and attempting to discover a nonce that will make this new puzzle accurate. This process takes place within the new block. When this new block is located, the block that comes after it uses a portion of the block that came before it, and so on. When a new block is added, it always goes on top of the one that came before it on the stack; this is how the numbering system works.

WORTH NOTING

When it comes to cryptography, a blockchain is created when all of the blocks are linked together to form one continuous chain.

The initial block that is added to a blockchain is referred to as the "genesis block." On January 3, 2009, Satoshi launched the cryptocurrency that bears his name. As of right now, there are tens of hundreds of thousands of blocks on top of it, all of which are linked together through cryptography. You were unable to modify any of the blocks in the middle since doing so would have rendered the blockchain useless after that block. This is a very critical point to make clear before moving further with our discussion of the immutability of a blockchain. If you wanted to alter the past, you would have to delete all of the subsequent blocks (puzzles) and begin the process from the beginning. If you alter just a single transaction, the whole block of riddles, as well as all of the puzzles that come after it, will be impacted as a result. Almost without exception, the amount of work required to edit the blockchain is outweighed by the benefits that may be reaped from doing so.

WORTH NOTING

For this reason, a blockchain is seen as an unchangeable history of transactions that may be agreed upon by a decentralized community.

When it comes to Bitcoin, a transaction is regarded as being immutable when it has been confirmed four or five times, provided that three to four more blocks are on top of it. This process typically takes between 40 and 50 minutes. A transaction in Bitcoin is considered to be reasonably safe even if it is only verified once, particularly if the value being transacted is less than a certain threshold. Who would spend a few thousand dollars on computer time to mine a new block simply to steal a few bucks from you? These are the costs associated with creating a new block. If you don't have any economically savvy pals, you shouldn't even try to justify doing it to yourself. As a general rule, owing to cryptography, a Bitcoin transaction that involves hundreds of thousands of dollars is regarded unchangeable after it has been confirmed by a minimum of four or five other transactions.

WORTH NOTING

Keep in mind that regardless of the currency we use, we must always ask ourselves why we trust that particular money to be a reliable unit of account, medium of transfer, and store of value. In the first chapter, we went through this topic as follows: The tale of gold. Fiat is Italian for "central authority." In other words, cryptography.

Because it is very difficult to outwork the other members of the group, the stability of a cryptocurrency naturally improves as the number of individuals that engage in it grows. When there are just ten individuals involved in a cryptocurrency, it is extremely vulnerable; but, just picture the situation if there were millions of people involved, as is the case with Bitcoin. It packs a significant punch. There are times when different groups have opposing viewpoints. If two miners discover the same block at about the same time, this is one of the scenarios in which this might take place.

A Look At The Pros And Cons Of Day Trading

Aspects that are favorable

1. the opportunity of generating substantial gains Day trading's most enticing feature is the prospect of obtaining great profits, which may be made by participating in the activity. However, this may only be a possibility for the exceptionally rare person who possesses all of the characteristics — definitiveness, discipline, and perseverance — that are essential to become a great day trader.

2. Take charge of your own career: An autonomous worker who is insulated from the orders of high-ranking executives in major businesses is known as a day trader. He is free to pick his own working hours, take breaks whenever they are required, and go with his task at his own pace, in contrast to an employee who is bound to the tight timetable of a corporate treadmill. He also has the ability to take breaks whenever they are needed.

3. A flood of exhilaration that never seems to end: Day traders who have experience find

that putting their wits against those of the market and other industry pros during the course of each and every trading day gives them a rush of adrenaline that they find exhilarating. Even though it is a significant factor in why they choose to make their living through trading as opposed to, say, spending their days selling electronic devices or laboring over figures in an office setting, very few brokers would admit to the rush of adrenaline that comes from rapid-fire trading. This is despite the fact that it is one of the primary reasons why they choose to make their living through trading.

4. Expensive training is not required; in many financial careers, all that is required for meetings is to have the relevant degree from the appropriate college. Because of this, there is no longer a need for costly training. It is important to highlight that one does not require an expensive degree from an Ivy League school in order to participate in day trading. Even though there are no mandated educational prerequisites to become a day trader, you may discover that attending a few classes in specialized research or digital trading would be beneficial to your career.

5. The benefits of going into business for oneself Due to the fact that a day trader is considered to be an independently employed worker, they are eligible to deduct certain expenses when filing their taxes. This is something that a person who is now employed is unable to promise.

The Market For Cryptocurrency

Acquiring Knowledge on Cryptocurrency
To put it succinctly, bitcoin is an innovative kind of digital currency. Although traditional currencies that are not based on blockchain technology, such as the US dollar, can be transferred digitally, the process is not the same as that used by cryptocurrencies. When cryptocurrencies reach a point where they are accepted by a larger number of people, you might be able to use them to make electronic payments in the same way that you can use conventional currencies.

However, what sets cryptocurrencies apart from traditional currencies is the underlying blockchain technology. "Who cares about the technology underlying my money?" you might be wondering. The only thing that concerns me is how much of it is now in my wallet! The problem is that the current monetary systems all over the world have a lot of problems that need to be fixed. The following are some illustrations:

The use of credit cards and wire transfers as methods of payment is now considered archaic.

The majority of the time, a plethora of middlemen, such as banks and brokers, take a cut of the action, which increases the cost of transactions and extends the amount of time it takes to complete them.

The discrepancy in wealth that exists across the world is widening.

About three billion people worldwide do not have bank accounts, either because they do not have enough money or because they do not use banks. That is equivalent to about half of the total population of the globe!

The use of cryptocurrencies is an attempt to overcome a number of these problems, if not all of them entirely.

Acquiring A Knowledge Of The Fundamentals
You are aware that the banks hold the money that is regularly issued by the government. And that in order to obtain more of it or transfer it to other people, you are required

to have access to a bank or an ATM. The use of cryptocurrencies, on the other hand, may make it possible to completely eliminate the need for banks and other centralized middlemen. The reason for this is that blockchain, a decentralized technology, is what underpins cryptocurrencies. This means that there is no central authority overseeing blockchain. Instead, every computer that is part of the network is responsible for verifying the transactions.

Bitcoin's adaptable problem space.

The fact that people have different cutoff points for the maximum number of transactions that the bitcoin network may alter is the root cause of the bitcoin scalability problem. It is possible that this is a result of the guarantee that each block in the blockchain is limited to a particular case megabyte carried out measure. Since the mosscup oak late squares have a solid purpose to be generated, bitcoin squares have been used to pass on the transactions that individuals have made using the bitcoin framework. In the same way that limited should further strengthen The individuals' bitcoin network's hypothetical greatest capacity stands in the center of 3. 3 and 7 transactions to each second, which is significantly lower than Visa's top banana, which claims to process 47,000 transactions per second.

The one megabyte limit that individuals must adhere to has caused a bottleneck in bitcoin, which has resulted in something similar to rising transaction costs. In addition to what has been acknowledged, you should be prepared for transactions that will not fit within a square. Approaches that are unique to the proposals are shown. When it came to the question of how bitcoin will be scaled, another aggressive common argument needed to go something like this. This discussion was based on the profits made by certain business insiders in 2017, Also The same might be said of a "ideological conflict once more regarding bitcoin's future." In regard to the 21st of July 2017, bitcoin miners that were locked into a result redesign were referred to as needing extra strengthening. In relation to the outline Bitcoin Improvement Proposal 91 (BIP 91), which stipulates that anyone who are unsure should detach from the network. Throughout the entirety of square 477,120, witness redesign was started.

Bitcoin's Beginnings As A Concept

Bitcoin is a sort of digital currency, which means that it is created digitally and stored digitally as well. This is out of everyone's hands at this point. Bitcoins, in contrast to paper currency, are not printed; rather, they are generated by individuals and other enterprises that have electronic operations in different parts of the world. The production of Bitcoins, however, takes use of software that assists in the solution of mathematical problems.

This is the very first example of a form of money that will soon be part of an emerging category known as cryptocurrency.

What is the main difference?

Bitcoin is a digital currency that may be used to make online purchases. In this regard, they are relatively comparable to traditional fiat currencies such as the dollar or the euro, both of which are also exchanged digitally, such as the dollar or the euro.

The fact that Bitcoin is not managed by a single institution or central authority is its defining feature, as well as the one that differentiates it from traditional forms of currency. There is not a single organization that possesses the ability to exercise complete command over the Bitcoin network. Because their financial stability is not dependent on the decisions made by huge financial institutions, this may be appealing to certain individuals.

Who was the creator of it?

Satoshi Nakamoto, a programmer, was the one who initially came up with the concept of a bitcoin. This was an electronic payment system that was founded on several mathematical calculations. The goal of developing this system was to come up with a type of money that could function without any oversight from a governing body whatsoever, yet could still be sent from one person to another via the internet in an instant and at a very minimal cost.

Who would be willing to print it?

The good news is that nobody would have to print it. Due to the fact that this is not produced in physical form by a central bank, it is not answerable to the general public and operates under its own unique set of guidelines. In general, banks have the ability to produce additional money, which might be used to cover their national debt; but, this would result in a devaluation of their currency. Instead, Bitcoins are generated digitally through a process known as "mining," which is open to participation from anybody. Mining for bitcoin is accomplished through the usage of a decentralized network. This network not only assists in the processing of transactions that may be conducted using virtual money, but it also allows Bitcoin to function as its own payment network.

The Ethereum Coin

The money known as ether is what gives the Ethereum blockchain its strength. Solidity is the name of the programming language used by the Ethereum network.

Ethereum, a decentralized blockchain network, is utilized in order to verify and record transactions. On the Ethereum platform, users may develop applications, publish them for usage by others, monetise those applications, and utilize those applications themselves; payments are conducted using the cryptocurrency Ether. A consensus has been reached among industry experts that dApps are decentralized apps running on the network.

As of May 2021, Ethereum has the second-highest value among all cryptocurrencies on the market, and it was behind Bitcoin by a very narrow margin.

It is reported that Ethereum is an open-source platform that is built on blockchain and that it is used to construct and share applications for various industries, including business, financial services, and entertainment.

dApps on Ethereum require users to pay fees referred to as "gas." They differ depending on the amount of processing power that is required.

Ether, sometimes abbreviated as ETH, is the digital asset that is used to transact on the Ethereum blockchain.

Ethereum's value currently ranks second only to that of Bitcoin among all of the market's cryptocurrencies.

Acquiring Knowledge About Ethereum

Users are able to utilize smart contracts and distributed apps (dApps) without the risk of being interrupted, scammed, or interfered with by a third party because the primary objective behind the development of Ethereum was to provide developers with the tools necessary to construct and publish safe and secure versions of these types of applications.

According to Ethereum's official description, it is "the world's programmable blockchain." Being a programmable network with the purpose of providing a secure and risk-free marketplace for the sale of software, games, and financial services. The fact that payment may be made in Ether is one of the things that sets Ethereum apart from Bitcoin.

The People Who Created Ethereum

In July of 2015, a small group of blockchain fanatics led by Vitalik Buterin and Joe Lubin, the founder of blockchain applications developer ConsenSys, established Ethereum. Vitalik Buterin is credited with coming up with the concept of Ethereum, and he currently functions as Ethereum's CEO and public face. Joe Lubin is also a member of the Ethereum team. Buterin, who was born in 1994, is frequently referred to as the youngest cryptocurrency billionaire in the world. Even though it was supposed to be used only within the Ethereum network, Ether is currently a method of payment that is accepted by a number of businesses and service providers. These include online retailers and service providers such as Overstock, Shopify, and CheapAir.

What exactly is the acronym ETH?

The transactional token known as Ether makes it easier to carry out operations on the Ethereum network. The applications and services that are linked with the Ethereum network require computational power, which is not provided for free. Payment for the ability to carry out actions on the network is made through the use of ether.

It is often understood that Ether is the coin that drives the Ethereum blockchain;

however, a more accurate description of Ether is that it is the "fuel" of this network. Ether is responsible for tracking and facilitating each and every transaction that takes place on the network. Although this is not how a typical cryptocurrency operates, Ether does have several characteristics with other cryptocurrencies like bitcoin, including the fact that it can be mined.

The transactional currency known as Ether is what drives all of the operations that take place on the Ethereum blockchain.

Blockchain development is utilized by Ethereum technology, which is utilized by third-party internet firms, in order to alter the storage of client data such as bank records.

As of the year 2021, Ether has surpassed Litecoin to become the second-largest virtual currency by market capitalization, trailing only Bitcoin.

In 2017, development work began on Ethereum 2.0, also known as the transition of the Ethereum network from a proof-of-work (PoW) system to a proof-of-stake (PoS) system. Ethereum 2.0 is not yet completely built and has not been deployed.

What Is The Function Of Bitcoin?

The function of Bitcoin has been discussed in detail: A worldwide currency that is decentralized and uses a peer-to-peer transaction mechanism to eliminate the need for middlemen (such as banks, payment applications, and so on). The transaction costs are lower. So let's assume a person spends their money for one bitcoin. What applications do they find for it? There is no limit to the possibilities. BTC is involved in everything from purchasing groceries to investing in and financing businesses to funding investments in businesses. This chapter will assist you grasp what exactly would be the use in owning or even getting associated with BTC by peeling back the layers into what those components are and educating you on what exactly would be the benefit of doing so.

Companies in business

On the website that is officially associated with Bitcoin, there is a link that leads to a list of the many ways in which a company may advance its interests by purchasing and accepting Bitcoin. Bitcoin's (BTC) long-term objective is not only to serve as a medium of exchange, but rather as a genuine form of hard capital for use by commercial enterprises.

When you accept Bitcoin as payment, you do not have to be concerned about the risk of payment fraud, in contrast to using a platform like PayPal. Because Bitcoin uses a public ledger, it is impossible for anybody to take back payments made using Bitcoin. Even very modest enterprises, such as clothing firms, typically have a global customer base for their products. When using Bitcoin, there is no need to wait for international transfers and there are no additional costs associated with taking money from other countries. If you accepted Bitcoin as payment, you wouldn't have to worry about charging customers additional fees, which would free up more of your time to concentrate on growing your business.

The first thing to take into consideration when thinking about incentives for companies and enterprises to invest in BTC is transparency. This is true whether it is for the purpose of accounting or for the acquisition of goods and services that a company requires. BTC was designed with a feature called multi-signature that enables only a select set of people to validate payments. To put it another way, there is no need to be concerned about members of a corporation spending money without the register's permission.

Purchases Made Independently

The modern world holds the promise of a future in which it will be possible to make purchases using contactless technology and that paper money and metal coins will be obsolete. One of the many bright new things that started seeping out into our day-to-day lives is Bitcoin (BTC), as well as cryptocurrencies more generally.

One of the primary individual applications for Bitcoin ever since it was created is making purchases over the internet in other countries. If there was just one currency used everywhere, then everyone would be aware of its value and profits, and national boundaries wouldn't matter when it came to shopping. In the future, we will see individuals paying for services and food using Bitcoin (BTC) since payment networks will accept Bitcoin as a valid form of currency.

But how would it work if one bitcoin is currently worth hundreds of dollars? How do people typically divide it up?

There are multiple'splitting' options available for Bitcoin. Because Bitcoin is not something that can be physically divided, the expression is expressed with quotation marks. It's not even a fraction of a penny on the dollar. Bitcoins themselves are not stored anywhere;

but, a ledger of all of their transactions is. That transaction's key is held by a certain individual. That indicates that you are able to purchase one Bitcoin. Or fifty percent of it.Alternately, a quarter.Or 0.00000001 percent of it. What this individual would have is the ownership of the'splitting' of the asset. These quantities are referred to as fractions of BTC. One hundred millionth of a bitcoin is the lowest amount of BTC that a person may hold. In recognition of the person who devised this unit of currency, we name it a Satoshi.

Because Bitcoins can be divided into smaller units, the uses for them are virtually limitless. It would sound strange to have to continually divide up money, but it wouldn't be all that unlike from having to deal with a finite quantity of pennies and dividing them out in accordance with their value.

How To Safely Preserve Your Cryptocurrency Holdings

Despite the fact that cryptocurrencies exist only in digital form, they are nonetheless considered to be money. They have the same amount of worth. Therefore, you should store them in a secure location, just as you would with money that is physically held in your possession. After all, you wouldn't just leave your wallet sitting around somewhere haphazardly, would you?

So, how exactly can you guarantee the safety and protection of your cryptocurrency holdings?

You will need to create a digital wallet if you intend to invest in cryptocurrencies in the future. It is essentially the same as the wallet that you carry with you, with the exception that it is digital. Only in the realm of digital data does it exist. You may save this wallet on a variety of devices and connect it to a bank account at the same time.

You need to be on guard at all times since there are many dishonest people and hackers on the internet. Your cryptocurrency may be taken from you if you are careless about its storage. You absolutely must have access to a trustworthy wallet in order to store your digital currency. Wallets for cryptocurrencies are pieces of software that not only hold public and private keys for interacting with various blockchains, but also store the keys themselves.

You are able to transmit cryptocurrencies, receive them, and keep track on their balances. Additionally, there is a selection of wallets available for your consideration. In an ideal world, you would pick the one that caters most closely to your requirements. For instance, you have the option of becoming an active trader, a passive investor who simply buys and holds, or a combination of the two. You will be able to start buying and selling digital currencies on multiple platforms as soon as you have finished setting up your digital wallet and are ready to do so.

Keeping Cryptocurrencies in Cold Storage

Your cryptocurrency can be stored in a number of different ways, including the following:

The trading of

The most user-friendly and straightforward method for storing digital currency is via an exchange. After all, this is the place where transactions involving such money take place. However, if you do decide to keep your coins in an exchange, you need to be aware that the exchange is not regulated in any way. Because it is easily hacked, it does not provide a particularly high level of security.

at point of fact, I won't suggest that you keep your digital currency at an exchange because I don't think it's a good idea. Unless, of course, you add additional layers of protection such as a two-factor authentication in addition to a password. This would be the recommended course of action.

You may also utilize Google Authentication to guarantee that your information is kept secure, even in the event that an attacker replicates your mobile device and uses it to access your account. In addition, if you want an extra layer of protection for your money, you can choose to have them kept in a cold storage facility.

Cold Wallet, also known as an Online Wallet

Keeping your digital currency in an online wallet, as opposed to an exchange, offers a higher level of security. To add insult to injury, this is not the safest method. Even so, it may still be susceptible to hacking. In addition, there are further prerequisites to meet. Therefore, if you are a person who is constantly on the go, you can discover that the processes are time-consuming.

However, you should schedule time in your schedule for these operations if you want to ensure the safety of your digital money. You should, ideally, establish a number of online wallets for your use. By doing so, your cryptocurrency will be dispersed among many accounts, reducing the likelihood that it would be taken all at once by a hacker who gains access to your wallet despite your precautions.

There are a few different options available to you when it comes to stowing away your cryptocurrency in an online wallet. To begin, you have the option of selecting a wallet that encrypts both your private and public keys and keeps them online. Second, you have the option of selecting a wallet that saves your private keys on your own computer or mobile device.

Let's say you make the decision to keep your cryptocurrency in a cloud wallet. Because you have private keys, your coins won't be vulnerable to theft if they are stored on your own computer. However, if a virus were to sneak into your computer, they may be vulnerable to being hacked.

You may save your coins in a mobile wallet, such as Jaxx, if you prefer to use your smartphone instead of a traditional wallet. This mobile wallet can sync with both your smartphone and your personal computer, allowing you to safely store backup copies of your private keys on both devices. It is possible to store a variety of cryptocurrencies, including Bitcoin, Litecoin, and Ethereum, amongst others, in this digital wallet.

Tokens That Cannot Be Destroyed

NFTs are the most well-known kind of the smart contract family. In general, a non-fiat currency (NFT) functions exactly the opposite way that a cryptocurrency does. Fungibility is an inherent property of every form of cryptocurrency. To put it another way, your bitcoin and my bitcoin are both equivalent in terms of the amount of fiat currency that they are worth, which implies that it is simple for us to swap one for the other. NFTs are not fungible in any way. Since each NFT is, in essence, one of a kind, it is impossible to swap one for another since they each have their own individual worth on the market. In the real world, the vast majority of the possessions we have cannot be exchanged for anything else. Your automobile and mine are both cars, but you cannot trade them for each other since they are different models. This is also the case with homes, the majority of apparel, and the majority of jewels.

The two most popular standards for NFTs are smart contracts that are written in Ethereum's programming language and stored on the blockchain:

A standard interface for non-fungible tokens, commonly known as deeds and denoted by the codename ERC-721.

ERC-1155 is an industry-standard interface for use in contracts that manage a variety of token kinds. Any combination of fungible tokens, non-fungible tokens, or other configurations (such as semi-fungible tokens, for example) may be used in a single deployed contract. Other configurations may also be used.

NFTs are produced (also known as "minted") when a one-of-a-kind token together with an accompanying smart contract is recorded on a blockchain. In principle, NFTs cannot be exchanged for other assets. To phrase it another way, the NFT of Nyan Cat is one of a kind and cannot be used interchangeably with other copies of the same file because it was purchased at auction for around $560,000. Here, you can find a list of prominent websites that allow you to mint your own NFTs.

Developing Fans and Audiences Through the Use of NFTs

People have begun to use the word "digital collectible" interchangeably with the term "NFT," which stands for "not for trade." It is a shame that this is the case since, despite the fact that the majority of the digital collectibles that have been in the news recently have been NFTs, there are numerous other ways in which technology may be utilized to produce value. If we consider the concept of "fan or audience development," which we will describe as a set of purpose-built tools with the intention of expanding communities of interest, the most apparent use for a non-fungible token (NFT) is probably as a ticket to an event. Let's go over some of the advantages that could be available to you if you combine a smart contract, some one-of-a-kind digital assets, and a ticket.

Smart Contracts are referred to as NFTs.

Every every NFT is a smart contract. A smart contract is quite similar to an old-fashioned verbal or written contract; the only difference is that with a smart contract, the agreement is automatically put into effect (digitally) after the requirements have been satisfied. The ability to create contracts that are immutable and self-executing, in conjunction with the automated exchange of monies (or tokens), opens up a world of possibilities for ticketing. The Removal of Any False or Unauthorized Tickets

Every non-fungible token is one of a kind, and ownership is recorded on a public distributed ledger known as a blockchain, which anyone may access and read. If the ownership of an NFT has been verified, a rapid comparison of public and private keys (using something as simple as a barcode scanner) would quickly verify that the person possessing the NFT in their digital wallet was the legitimate owner of the ticket. This would be the case even if the ownership of the NFT had previously been questioned.

Earnings from Third-Party Marketplaces

If someone buys an NFT ticket, the transaction can trigger royalty payments to the issuer as well as any other stakeholder, including musicians, sports leagues, players, sponsors, promoters, a charity, or virtually anyone with a digital wallet. These payments can be made simultaneously. These business rules may be hard-coded into each NFT, and just as with other smart contracts, when a transaction takes place and the requirements are satisfied, the money are immediately transferred from one party to another.

Benefits Of Digital Currency

Current Cryptocurrency Expansion
In 2012, WordPress was the first significant business to take bitcoin payments. Then came others like Newegg.com, Microsoft, and Expedia.
Benefits of Digital Currency
• Inherent scarcity: The number of units that can ever exist is specified in the source code of cryptocurrencies. Because they are designed to be scarce, these electronic currencies resemble precious metals more than traditional money. Similar to precious metals, cryptocurrencies provide an inflation hedge that holders of fiat money cannot obtain.
• Lack monopoly over government currency: Cryptocurrencies provide a trustworthy method of exchange that is not under the direct supervision of national banks like the US Federal Reserve and the European Central Bank. Those who worry about long-term economic instability due to the government's loose monetary policy may find this especially appealing. Numerous economists and political scientists predict that different

governments may appropriate cryptocurrencies or integrate their features—like built-in scarcity and authentication procedures—into standard currencies.

• Communities that are self-interested and self-policing: Mining is a built-in quality control and policing mechanism for cryptocurrencies. Young people get paid for their work. Thus, they maintain an accurate and up-to-date record. This protects the system's integrity and the value of the money.

• Robust privacy protections: Early proponents of cryptocurrencies were primarily concerned with anonymity and privacy, and they remain so today. A lot of bitcoin users use aliases that are distinct from any accounts, details, or saved data that might be used to identify them. Advanced community members could be able to figure out who the users are. More safeguards in post-bitcoin or more recent cryptocurrencies make it considerably more challenging.

•Out of government control: States have the authority to intercept financial transactions conducted in neighboring nations or to freeze or confiscate domestic bank accounts. The decentralized nature of cryptocurrencies, on the other hand, means that governmental seizure attempts are thwarted because transaction histories and money are kept in multiple locations throughout the globe.

• Generally less expensive than analog electronic transactions: The issue of duplicate spending is successfully resolved by the wallets, block keys, and private keys. Security makes sure that novices in the bitcoin space aren't taken advantage of by seasoned users who can replicate virtual currency. With cryptocurrencies, every electronic financial transaction can be verified and authenticated without the assistance of a third party like PayPal or Visa. Therefore, there is no longer a requirement for required transaction fees. Typically, transition fees for cryptocurrencies are less than 1% of the transition value. However, 3% is taken by credit card and PayPal.

• Less expense and barrier for cross-border transitions: Cryptocurrencies, in contrast to domestic transitions, handle international transitions in the same way. Either there is no fee associated with the transaction, or there is one. No matter where the source and recipient of the money are located. This is a significant benefit over international transactions using common currency. There is usually an ATM or credit card fee when traveling abroad.

How To Profit From Cryptocurrency Trading

You may begin trading cryptocurrencies immediately with just a few dollars' worth of Bitcoin. There aren't any broker fees, middlemen to deal with, entry barriers, or red tape in reality. All you require is a fraction of a single Bitcoin. There is no reason not to give it a try. It's a great way to get into cryptocurrency if you can tolerate risking a few dollars.

I began trading with less than $40 in Bitcoin.

In less than a month or two, I worked my way up to 5.5 Bitcoin (worth over $5,000 at the time). This is not meant to imply that trading is simple or straightforward. While losing money is an inevitable part of trading and investing, you may minimize risk and losses by using the appropriate tactics. The truth is that everyone would trade if it were a simple, risk-free method of making money. Trading cryptocurrency, however, will suit you if you're a patient, strategically minded individual who can also study market trends.

The true Occupy Wall Street is cryptocurrency.

As a decentralized leader, the Blockchain cannot be managed or controlled by a single institution. Its design renders transactions virtually error-proof. Furthermore, it is capable of far more than merely transferring ownership of digital currency; it can be employed for the transfer of assets and shares of businesses, smart contracts, commodities, and equity services. This technology will probably transform finance as we know it in the future by demarcating financial markets and getting rid of "banksters."

In the beginning stages of learning cryptography, the technical jargon may appear overwhelming.

While learning is important, for the time being, if you're just getting started in trading and investing, having a basic understanding of business, consumer demand, and economics will offer you an advantage over other traders. The majority of today's traders are early adopters of bitcoin, "miners" of cryptocurrencies, programmers, and, generally speaking, more tech-savvy than business- or market-savvy.

They concentrate on little technological advancements that aid in creating hype for a coin in the near future, but they don't address much regarding the coin's existence after changes and cryptocurrency. You gain a great advantage from this.

So let's get going. Purchase some Bitcoin first.

While certain exchanges allow you to purchase certain cryptocurrency for US dollars, it's advisable to get Bitcoin first. You can trade into and out of every other cryptocurrency on the market, on every cryptocurrency exchange, using a bit of Bitcoin. Remember that you don't have to acquire Bitcoin in its whole ($390 at the time of writing); instead, you can buy it in fractions known as Satoshis, where 500k Satoshis is equivalent to 0.005 Bitcoin. Coinbase is the most popular and secure way to buy Bitcoin.In addition, you might visit an exchange that offers a USD-BTC parity in order to try and swap USD for Bitcoin at a more favorable rate.

Now that you own some Bitcoin, it's time to locate an exchange.

The most trustworthy change I've discovered is Bittrex.com. Other exchanges exist; some are good, some are bad, others have already been shut down (you may remember the Mt. Gox fiasco). When news breaks about an exchange closing or coins being stolen, some people become angry about cryptocurrency altogether, but I see all of this as a part of growth for any new market that is still in its infancy. The fact that the majority of these hopeful exchanges have been terminated and their CEOs have been exposed and sued extensively is incredibly heartening.

In the crypto world, news spreads quickly, so be sure to check the feeds daily.

As long as you pay attention to the news on Twitter, you will typically see smoke before there is a fire. Businesses and cryptocurrency exchanges are being discussed on Twitter. Every day, check in on Twitter and cryptocurrency forums, follow hash tags, and see what others are talking about. News is news, information is information, and rumors are opportunities!

Trading can begin once you have Bitcoin in your exchange account.

But before you randomly select some cryptocurrency and examine its charts, I advise you to conduct some research first; if not, you'll be trading without thinking. To learn more about each coin, search for it online using terms like "Cannabiscoin Ann" (with the "ann" standing for announcement). This search term will take you to the official announcement thread of Bitcoin on the bitcointalk.org forums.

Basic trading.

The process of reexamining the market is known as "fundamental analysis." It becomes easier to maintain trend predictions by obtaining the appropriate information at the appropriate time and comprehending how it will interact with the market, including whether or not a cryptocurrency will rise or fall. Apart from fundamental analyses, you also possess "technical analyses." Technical analysis is also important, but it specifically refers to studying charts and identifying patterns—for instance, a coin will fall regularly at a given price.

So, What Kind Of Security Software Is Required?

It is not enough to simply download any free antivirus program and call yourself safe. Antivirus software has to have updates delivered on a regular basis by a committed team of experts. Those teams are expensive. The villains are never tired. Here, you cannot afford to select "free."

 Buying an antivirus product should not be done by a corporation that tracks and sells your data for profit—this is how free protection solutions fund malware research teams. Big Brother is living on your computer, even if their software is good at snaring nasty stuff. That cannot be done.

BitDefender, Malware Bytes Premium, or Kaspersky. Malware Bytes has a free version,however it's not quite good enough if you want to safeguard your priceless Ethereum and Bitcoins. The free version merely an infection scanner that detects damage to the machine after it has already occurred.

A blacklist of questionable websites is updated in real time in the premium edition. The software will terminate the connection if you try to access a restricted website, which will prevent you from viewing the compromised page. While you can use your regular desktop computer to browse the web, you shouldn't be doing it on your cryptocurrency virtual machine.

You solely use the VM to manage your finances. That is all!

A bank-useful sandboxed browser is included with Eset. When you wish to trade, you can use it to disable all plugins, which are quite helpful for connecting to the exchanges.

Additionally, Eset is available in Linux and Mac versions. Malware and viruses may also infiltrate both of the systems. They too will need to be safeguarded.

Finally, let me say this: if you use Windows, be aware that it is surreptitiously eavesdropping on you all the time. It keeps returning telematic data to Microsoft. Spybot Anti-Beacon is a free tool that needs to be downloaded in order to stop surveillance engines.

A Windows machine can be secured using certain system administrator approaches. The optimal method involves deleting your user permissions from the registry keys, enabling Windows to launch certain applications.

It won't start it up, even if there is malware and it tries to install itself. The installation of the program will be prevented since you are not executing it as an administrator. The machine would only be permitted to autoinstall when it has been identified and is operating in administrator mode. Thus, ensure that this is not how your machine is configured. You can set it to Admin if you need to install and configure authentic software, but remember to change it back when you're done. There is a small issue while installing authentic software, however you can adjust permissions, install the program, and then adjust permissions to their initial configurations. Lastly, you must remove erratic software from your computer right now. Make sure no search bars or browser plugins are installed, and there shouldn't be any installed web games.

"Making ten or fifteen times as much money doesn't necessarily follow from having ten or fifteen plays at once. It's highly likely that you will become distracted, make mistakes, and produce nothing.

You should treat the procedure with the same seriousness as the money you are risking, which entails monitoring the chart where your cash are kept. You will probably miss out on the crucial hints that the pricing is providing you if you have too many plays open at once.

Any chart that needs to be watched should have its levels clearly spelled out. You would be able to adjust your risk amount based on these levels. You risk missing a crucial signal if you are preoccupied with something else, which may be a very expensive error.

"My suggestion would be to focus on a limited selection of plays if you are struggling to trade. As you become comfortable with a chart, your intuition will take over.

Trading distractions can also arise from having too many charts open at once.

Assume for the moment that you and your buddies are watching your favorite sports team play and you decide to make a deal. After a few minutes, you lose yourself in the game and neglect to check the chart. It plummeted another 10% while you were away and broke through a critical support level. What a calamity!

"Those who view trading as a pastime will soon need to find another one."

Trading while intoxicated or under the influence of drugs might land you in hot water in addition to having an excessive number of charts open or becoming sidetracked while watching sports. You should treat money with respect when it's involved. That entails abstaining from alcohol in order to maximize your chances of making a profitable trade.

An overabundance of attention to long-term price projections is another prevalent cause of distraction for individuals. You are diverting your attention from the present situation when you consider where the price might go in the future. You are more likely to overlook certain hints from the current price action if you adopt that position.

"Pay attention to what your favorite play is saying you about supply and demand right now, and stop speculating about what it will cost at the end of the year. Do more watching and less forecasting.

How To Buy Nft

The NFT market has had a rapid rise in value during the last three years, expanding by almost 10 times between 2018 and 2020. The market capitalization of the NFT market increased from $40.96 million to $141.56 in 2019 and then soared to $338.04 in 2020. As a result of the NFT market's rapidly increasing market capitalization, celebrities, venture capitalists, big investors, and other prominent figures have started to show interest in participating in the NFT action.

In addition to the NFT industry's rapidly increasing market capitalization, nonfungible.com—which monitors NFT data across more than 120 NFT marketplaces—states that the total number of NFTs sold to date is 5.48 million, bringing in $542,474,788 in income! This total revenue divided by four years equals an average of $135,618,697 annually, indicating that the average annual sales volume from NFT sales is approximately $135 million!

Even yet, I think there is still a lot of room for growth in the NFT sector, especially given that the $135 million in sales volume annually is a small portion of the $63.7 billion in sales volume produced by traditional art marketplaces. If I had to estimate the yearly sales volume that the NFT marketplace will produce within the next ten years, I would say that it will be 10% of the yearly volume of the traditional art marketplace. This implies that NFT's annual sales might easily reach $6.3 billion in the next ten years!

With an estimated yearly sales volume of $6.3 billion, Beeple's $69 million greatest NFT sale each day will not even come close to representing 0.01% of the total expected sales volume. Consider the implications for NFT sales in the future. This implies that NFT sales in the million zone will be typical for the NFT market.

Blockchain Technology And Its Effect On Traditional Financial Systems' Future

One of the most contentious subjects of the twenty-first century is blockchain technology. Blockchain is the way of the future, but not everyone agrees with this viewpoint; others criticize it and doubt its validity.

Since you are mulling over the possibility of making an investment in cryptocurrencies, it is only natural that you would be curious about the trajectory that blockchain technology and its progeny, cryptocurrencies, may follow in the years to come.
Is it possible that we are witnessing a repeat of the dot-com bubble?
Since its introduction, blockchain technology has presented major financial organizations, central banks, and governments from across the world with a significant challenge to their status quo.
A good number of them have been forced to employ researchers and to collaborate closely with large businesses operating in the blockchain and cryptocurrency industries in order to get the knowledge necessary to

comprehend what it is all about and how it can affect the future.

There is one thing that can be said with certainty: the ripple generated by the bitcoin business is already beginning to affect them.

A select group of knowledgeable individuals have offered some perceptive forecasts on some of the ways in which the traditional financial industry is likely to be disrupted by the introduction of blockchain technology.

Blockchain technology may one day render banks obsolete. If this occurs, there will be no need for traditional financial institutions like banks.

Banks play a significant part in the regulation of monetary exchanges; for example, they check to make sure that Mr. A has sufficient funds to send to Mr. B, and then they transfer the funds directly from Mr. A's account to Mr. B's account.

However, the government regulates banks, and banks demand exorbitant fees for the services that they offer; however, all of this may be avoided by utilizing blockchain technology. Banks are subject to government regulation.

Nobody is in charge of the system, which means that nobody is in charge of determining the exchange rates, and there is no need for excessive transaction fees or bank tellers sticking their noses into anyone's business.

One of the factors that gives blockchain technology the potential to put an end to the conventional banking system is the fact that it provides users with the ability to transact in complete anonymity.

End of an Era for Multiple Stock Exchanges There are more than a dozen stock exchanges operating in the globe today, some of which are wealthier than the others. Additionally, there are a number of limitations on who may participate in certain markets.

On the other hand, thanks to the blockchain technology, everyone gets a piece of the pie.

Now, a centralized stock market may be established anywhere in the globe, and everyone who wants to can take part in it and reap the rewards.

The end of fiat currency and exchange rates Some nations or people are richer than others in today's world merely because their currencies are rated higher than the currencies of other nations. Everyone will not quite have an equal opportunity to succeed under these circumstances. Even if people in impoverished nations put forth more effort than their counterparts in other countries, they won't be able to compete with them since their currencies are not as highly valued.

Because there will no longer be a need for numerous currencies in the financial industry, blockchain technology and cryptocurrencies will create an environment in which everyone will compete on an equal playing field.

Death to Credit: This is a topic that is not going to sit well with a lot of people, but the blockchain technology does not precisely create allowances for credit facilities. Instead, everyone is allowed to spend just what they already own.

The manner that the system is organized at the present does not include any provisions for the supply of credit facilities; nonetheless, it is possible that technologies for credit facilities may be implemented in the future; however, this is not guaranteed.

In a nutshell, the blockchain technology and cryptocurrency will contribute to the decentralization of the global economy and simplify the process of conducting business for all parties involved, irrespective of location or citizenship.

Keeping this information in mind, you might be wondering: will the excitement around cryptocurrencies continue for a while? The future of cryptocurrency is an intriguing topic. Let's talk about that some more.

Why Should One Use Cryptocurrency Instead Of Traditional Money?

Protection Against Fraud

Using bitcoin allows companies to avoid the hassle of chargebacks, which are prevalent when payments are made using credit cards due to the impossibility of arbitrarily reversing cryptocurrency transactions. Because each transaction involving a cryptocurrency has to be validated by the network before it can be processed, it is impossible to make phony payments using cryptocurrencies. In addition, when you pay for products or services using cryptocurrencies, you do not reveal any of your financial information to the retailer. This is a significant benefit. When you take into consideration the fact that hackers have constantly made news for hacking into small and major organizations in order to steal the financial information of consumers, the significance of this point becomes even more apparent.

Transfer in an Instant

The movement of funds across international borders often takes a few of days. You may transfer money to virtually any region of the world in just a few minutes if you use cryptocurrencies. The case is the same for companies that are willing to take payments made by credit card. They are need to wait for the money to be deposited into their bank accounts, which can take anywhere from several days to up to a week in certain cases. When a transaction is completed using bitcoin, the money is immediately available to the owner of the firm.

Reduced or Even Eliminated Transaction
Fees

When dealing with traditional banks and organizations that handle payment processing, you will always be required to pay processing costs whenever you need to move cash or process payments. Users of cryptocurrencies are able to conduct transactions without having to pay any fees since cryptocurrencies do away with the need for third intermediaries. However, the creation and upkeep of cryptocurrency wallets is something that the majority of bitcoin users rely on other parties to do. Even though these digital currencies do charge a fee for their services, such fees are far lower than those charged by traditional financial institutions and payment processing firms.

Complete Command and Management of Your Account

You do not have complete control over your bank account whether you use traditional banks or computerized cash management services. The bank or other financial entity is the one who actually owns your account. Take, for example, the fact that PayPal owns your PayPal account and that you have no say in how it is used. If PayPal determines that you have used your account inappropriately in any way, they may choose to freeze all of the cash in the account without first contacting you about their decision. You are the one who is going to have to shoulder the responsibility of proving to them that you did not abuse the account in any way. On the other hand, using a cryptocurrency grants you complete ownership of your account as well as full control over it. You are the only one who can view the private and public addresses associated with your wallet. Your bitcoin wallet is completely under your control as a result of this.

Increased Confidentiality

Wallets for cryptocurrencies are not connected to users' personally identifiable information in any way. Individuals are able to conduct confidential monetary transactions with one another. You won't have to worry about anyone prying into your business when you use cryptocurrencies to conduct transactions since they are completely anonymous.

Open to each and every individual

Mobile devices that can connect to the internet are becoming increasingly common, particularly in industrialized countries. It is anticipated that there will be 4.7 billion people using mobile phones by the time 2017 comes to a close. The usage of mobile devices for conducting financial transactions is common among a significant portion of this population. This demographic is an ideal candidate for the adoption of bitcoin. Businesses who are willing to take bitcoin payments will get access to a massive new customer base as cryptocurrency gains wider acceptance.

When talking about cryptocurrencies, it is hard to avoid someone bringing up the subject of investing at some point. The questions are applicable to everyone: Should I make an investment? To what amount? Is it a good time to act now, or should I hold off? Have I completely missed the boat when it comes to investing? Which currencies should be added to one's portfolio? Where can I get them and how can I get them?

Typically, I evade these queries by pointing out that an introductory work is not the appropriate location to seek financial counsel. This allows me to avoid answering the questions directly. In most cases, I will then proceed to give my normal pieces of advise, which are as follows: 1) You should not invest in things that you do not understand, and 2) You should not spend money in bitcoin that you cannot afford to lose.

The vast majority of individuals feel dissatisfied after following that guidance. It is only normal to be fascinated on the issue, even if you don't really plan on investing in any cryptocurrencies at all; people are making hundreds, thousands, and millions of dollars trading cryptocurrency, so it is only reasonable to be curious on the topic. So, for those people who are interested in crypto and want to know what I believe, I will provide my view here.

But before we go into it, a caveat:

I would want to make it clear that I am not a professional financial or investment advice. This chapter simply contains broad recommendations. It has been crafted without taking into consideration your aims, your financial status, or your requirements in any way. Before you take any action based on this advise, you should evaluate whether or not it is suitable in light of your specific goals, financial condition, and requirements.

Let's get down to business now that that's out of the way.

The monetary systems that are discussed in this book were selected by me because I believed they were either historically significant, novel in their approach, or intriguing in their own right. It is not necessary for anything to be "interesting" or "innovative" in order for it to have a potential for tenfold or one hundredfold rises in value in the future. It is possible that "historical significance" refers to the fact that a certain currency has already won the competition. To summarize, you shouldn't consider the existence of an alternative coin in this book or any other book to be a recommendation to purchase that coin.

However, out of all of the currencies that have been reviewed in this article, there are a few that I would most certainly suggest to an investor whose financial goals and level of tolerance for risk were comparable to mine. The following are the ones that, if I were given a quantity of money and directed to buy some of the currencies described in this book, I would make it a point to acquire:

Bitcoin: Bitcoin is a well-established cryptocurrency that is regarded as a blue-chip investment. Any price that is less than ten thousand dollars strikes me as a good deal, and I believe there is still a lot of room for price appreciation. This is merely a two- to threefold gain in value from where it is currently, so although there is money to be earned, it most likely won't be the game-changing bonanza that some are hoping it would be.

Ethereum: The fiasco with the DAO, the hard-fork that was linked with it, plus my own inherent cynicism kept me away from Ethereum until very recently. That was a bad move on your part. After doing further research and seeing the actual capabilities of this platform, I came to the conclusion that, despite some initial difficulties, it is superior to Bitcoin and has even more potential for growth.

The majority of my currency holdings would be comprised of these two different currencies. These are the types of investments that fall under the "Buy and Forget" category. I anticipate that both of these coins will stay in circulation for a very long time and will continue to exhibit an upward trend. I have the self-assurance to disregard any temporary setbacks in value or changes in price, presuming that these occurrences were not brought on by a shift in the fundamentals of the currency. If China makes the decision to once again prohibit Bitcoin and its price plummets as a result, I would seize the opportunity to purchase some Bitcoin at a discount. That is the prudent thing to do. However, if the Bitcoin developers decide to remove the cap on the amount of coins, which is now set at 21 million BTC, I will immediately sell all of my

Bitcoins because this will fundamentally disrupt what makes Bitcoin valuable.

After I had established a sufficient holding in Bitcoin and Ethereum, I would next diversify my holdings by purchasing some amount of the privacy-centric alternative cryptocurrencies, such as Zcoin, Zcash, or Monero. I've noticed that privacy is becoming even more of a term recently, despite the fact that it has always been one of the most important aspects of bitcoin. Take note that I did not mention DASH in this discussion. I do not believe that DASH is a poor alternative cryptocurrency; nonetheless, its baggage is working against it. I'd rather put my money on one of the up-and-comers. Zcoin is a cryptocurrency that has my attention at the moment. However, I believe that in the end, only a select fraction of the currencies that are focused on privacy will be successful. Although it's possible that all of them will carry on existing and have some value, I don't think there is place for more than one "mainstream privacy coin." Because I have no idea which alternative coin it will be, this is not an investment that can be "bought and left alone." This investment strategy entails more of a "buy low and hold while watching for signals" approach. Even while it won't take much of anyone's time, it could be more than most individuals are willing to put in. That is not hard to comprehend. Not everyone has aspirations of becoming a trader, and not everyone has the time or interest to spend one hour every day reading about cryptocurrencies. Those individuals should concentrate on Bitcoin and Ethereum instead.

Last but not least, there are a few other currencies that I might not acquire right now but would absolutely be interested in learning more about in the future. They may be advantageous to invest in... but on the other hand, they could not. However, you should give them some consideration. These two cryptocurrencies are called IOTA and ARK. Each of them aims to deliver characteristics that are lacking in certain areas that are either unjustified or disregarded by the bitcoin industry. They are not the only ones with these goals, but they have demonstrated a greater commitment to marketing and/or development than the majority of their rivals.

Chain of blocks

Because you are the sender, every single one of the messages that you send will not only be sent to the address that you are sending it to, but you will also be sending it to all of the nodes in the network (through the six (or more) nodes that you are linked to). That one message would have been received by the entirety of the network in a matter of seconds at most. when the message is finally sent out onto the network after all of the other nodes have observed the procedure. The giver now has a lower total number of coins, whereas the recipient now has a greater total number of coins.

Just to give you an example:

Luis plans to give Francis one Bitcoin (BTC) as payment. Francis will start off by making a wallet and finding an address. He will be the only one who possesses that address, and he will be given a private key. On the other side, Luis, who already possesses his own address, Private Key, and Bitcoin in his wallet, will get Francis' address and will announce to the network that he will be transferring 1 BTC to Francis. Francis will then receive the Bitcoin. Luis already possesses his own address,

Private Key, and Bitcoin in his wallet. The message is going to be organized into blocks.

When a block has been successfully placed, the entire block is hashed, and then it is positioned next to the block. The miner will next make an attempt to unravel the mystery. The miner's hash will be included to the next batch of transactions when they have successfully solved the riddle. This process will continue until all of the puzzles have been solved.

A chain that cannot be broken will be produced as a result of this technique. After the transaction has been confirmed, there is no ability to undo or cancel it in any manner. Because any change in the hash, even a change in a single digit, will change the entire hash, it will never be changed again because the new hash will not be compatible with the hash that has already been stored.

The record will be stored on all of the nodes, which means that there will be thousands of recordings of this specific blockchain. This serves as proof that it cannot be altered in any way, and that this state of affairs will never change.

Although we just spent the most of our time talking about Bitcoin, some of the mechanisms that we discussed are applicable to other cryptocurrencies as well. The implementation is where the differences emerge, although they all share a similar principle at their core.

Its worth will be determined by the volume of coins that are wanted at any one moment compared to the amount of coins that are available, and both the value and the asset will become more fluid as a result of a dynamic market.

Trading in cryptocurrencies involves three distinct transactions: you may exchange fiat currencies for cryptocurrencies, or you can swap one cryptocurrency for another. The next section will provide you with further details on it.

How To Get Started Mining Bitcoins

In order to start mining Bitcoin, you'll need to get some Bitcoin mining hardware first. In the early days of Bitcoin, mining was feasible using either the central processing unit (CPU) of your computer or a high-speed video processing card. That is not possible in this day and age. Custom Bitcoin ASIC chips have come to dominate the Bitcoin mining industry as a result of their superior performance, which may be up to 100 times higher than that of earlier systems.

Mining Bitcoin together with anything else will cause you to use more electricity than you are likely to gain from the endeavor. It is absolutely necessary to mine Bitcoins using the best Bitcoin mining hardware that was developed exclusively for that use.

Many companies have begun producing chips that are only used for the operation of running the cryptographic algorithm. These chips are used only for the purpose. Antminer is a well-known piece of ASIC hardware that is utilized for mining Bitcoin. Antminer is available with a variety of "pecifications," such as U1 and U2+. U1 and U2+ both correspond to about the same zone. While the hash rate for U1 is set to 1.6 GH/s by default, the hash rate for U2+ is set to 2.0 GH/s. Wait for it: the process of entering Bitcoin transactions into the public ledger is referred to as. Mining for Bitcoin. Through the use of this procedure, they are brought into the system. The Bitcoin miner has the ability to make money off of transaction fees and subsidy for newly generated coins. A microchip that has been designed particularly for this procedure is known as an ASIC, which stands for application-specific integrated circuit. They are far quicker than the technologies that came before them. The Bitcoin miner provides a service that is determined by meeting certain performance standards. They offer a satisfactory level of manufacturing capability for the same price as other options.

If one has access to the appropriate data and resources, Bitcoin mining is not only profitable, but it's also an entertaining, risk-free method to move money across the internet. In other words, it's a triple threat. It is necessary to own both the appropriate software and powerful computer hardware in order to produce as much money as is possible.

The Prospects For Digital Currencies, Including Cryptocurrency

Money is unlike any other type of property in that it may be used for anything even before an event has taken place, making it a singular form of property. It doesn't imply anything, but it has the potential to be used for tremendous good or tremendous evil, and despite all the manipulation and influence it receives, it is still only what it is. It is a unique commodity, but one that is frequently misinterpreted and misused. Money has the simplicity of facilitating buying and selling, as well as a mathematical complexity, as shown by the financial markets; yet, it has no notion of egalitarianism, morality, or ethics in its decision making. It functions as an independent entity, despite the fact that it is both endogenous and exogenous to the international community. In spite of the fact that it lacks personality and is easily replaced, it is nonetheless seen as a finite resource in the context of the global economy, with its growth being governed by a set of complex rules that determine the manner in which it may function. Despite the fact that the results can never be predicted with absolute certainty, and despite the fact that a commitment to social justice and an aversion to moral turpitude are not prerequisites for its use, it is nevertheless a useful tool.

In order for a currency to effectively perform the financial functions required of it, the intrinsic value of money must be a commonly held belief by those who use it. If this is not the case, the currency will not be able to effectively fulfill the financial functions required of it.Many multinational corporations, venture capital firms, and individual investors from all over the world continue to attach a significant amount of importance to bitcoin in light of the cryptocurrency's growing popularity and widespread attention in the business sector.

Key Concepts Related To The Nft

NFTs have achieved such a degree of notoriety due to the celebrities that engaged in making, purchasing, and selling NFTs, as well as due to something that is fundamental to NFTs themselves, namely their capacity to produce value. You don't simply need to be familiar with the technology that NFTs are built on; in order to have a complete comprehension of what NFTs are, you need to have an understanding of a few fundamental ideas. The beauty of NFTs will become clear to you once you have this information, and you will be astounded by the influence they have on the lives of everyone and the path their lives take in the future.

In order to get a deeper comprehension of the matter at hand, we will get a grounding in the fundamentals, doing an in-depth analysis of each key concept.

In comparison to Subjective Value, Objective Value

People place importance on a wide variety of things, including goods themselves, experiences, hobbies, aspirations, vocations, and so on. If you were to ask a group of individuals what an experience or item is that is valuable to them, you would get a wide range of replies, which may include things like a beautiful walk on a dream beach, being with friends, listening to wonderful music, and many other things. The desire to have something is the unifying factor in all of these aspects. What is often regarded of as valuable is thought of in that way because there is an innate desire to get it or feel that it has been satisfied. We don't seek things, experiences, or anything else because of the sensation that they produce; rather, we desire things, experiences, and other things because of the passion that they generate. In addition, desire is the source of all subjective worth.

The idea of worth is intricately intertwined with preferences, which have a propensity to be arbitrary and are typically contingent upon what a particular individual believes, wishes, or observes. As long as we have desires, there will always be good reasons to search for pleasure. In addition to this, the satisfaction of more demands results in the creation of greater value. Therefore, subjective value is the worth that an individual is prepared to attribute to an item based on their own preferences and experiences. As a result, it is completely random and just transient. If you give it some thought, an immediate requirement might easily cause the worth of a product to skyrocket in comparison to what is typically or typically believed to be its value.

It is not as easy as one may think to define objective value. Even while we may speak of the transitory and non-arbitrary objectivity of prices (where a central power does not control the price of a thing), there is no realistic technique to evaluate value objectively. Prices can be temporary and not arbitrary objects. Therefore, if it were not for the coercion of an authority, every aspect of the matter would be entirely subjective. The price that is established by the market is the result of subjective judgments.

As a result, the value is not something that is inherently possessed by the product. It is not one of its qualities; rather, it is the significance that we attach to the fulfillment of our requirements about our existence and our well-being.

How To Get Your Hands On Some Cryptocurrency

There are two distinct ways to acquire cryptocurrency. The first method is to use fiat currency (such as USD, EUR, GBP, and so on) to buy cryptographic money through an exchange. The second method is to use private keys to obtain cryptocurrency. These deals follow a process that is analogous to that of standard trades involving unknown amounts of money. The prices are always fluctuating, and much like traditional cash trading marketplaces, they are open each and every day of the week. These transactions generate revenue by tacking on a nominal fee to each transaction that takes place.

While others impose fees solely on buyers, others tax both buyers and sellers for the privilege of transacting business. Before allowing you to acquire bitcoin, the majority of these exchanges will need you to verify your identity in order to comply with safety regulations. In addition to this, it is essential to take notice of the many types of payments that are accepted by each transaction. While some may only recognise payments made through PayPal or bank wires, some will accept payments made with credit cards and Visas. You may purchase Bitcoin, Ethereum, and other alternative cryptocurrencies using fiat currencies such as U.S. dollars, Euros, or British Pounds by using any of the following three money exchanges, which are the best and most reputable of their kind.

The Coinbase

Customers have the ability to buy, trade, and store digital currency on Coinbase, which is now the largest cryptocurrency marketplace anywhere in the world. Coinbase is without a doubt the easiest and most user-friendly exchange for beginners who are interested in becoming involved in the cryptocurrency industry. Once your identification has been confirmed, you'll be able to make a purchase of digital currency within Coinbase in a matter of minutes by using a bank account or debit card. Coinbase is a platform that allows users to trade several cryptocurrencies, including Bitcoin, Ethereum, and Litecoin, using fiat currency as the foundation.

Coinbase also offers a fully functional application for the iPhone and Android platforms, making buying and trading cryptocurrency in a hurry incredibly simple and quick. If you sign up for Coinbase by leveraging this connection, you will be eligible to get $10 worth of free Bitcoin after making your first purchase of cryptocurrency valued more than $100.

The Kraken

Kraken, which is based in Canada and is widely used for transactions denominated in Euros, has an advantage over Coinbase in that it supports a greater number of coins (in addition to allowing the purchase of Monero, Ethereum Classic, and Dogecoin).

You will need to have access to a market that facilitates the exchange of digital currency for cryptographic money in order to trade in other cryptocurrencies such as Dash and Golem.

Where Can I Find The Necessary Equipment To Begin Mining?

Obtaining or mining a cryptocurrency that operates via the proof-of-work approach is a little bit more difficult than other cryptocurrencies. Keep in mind that in order to mine for coins, you will need to solve a difficult computational task. Performing this operation not only confirms a transaction in a blockchain, but it also awards the miner a modest transactional fee for the work. This is appropriate, given that the miner does not personally solve the problem, but he is required to make a significant financial investment in a large amount of equipment that will efficiently complete the task.

The following are the components that may often be found in a miner's beginning pack:

1. Mining Equipment Made to Order

There was a time when all that was required to mine bitcoins was the Central Processing Unit (CPU) and the Graphics Processing Unit (GPU) of a desktop computer. In spite of the fact that people still have the option to do this, the vast majority of them do not since the entire process is impracticable. Using this sluggish equipment consumes an excessive amount of power, which means that doing so would cost almost as much as, or perhaps more than, the transaction fee that one would receive for successfully mining an issue.

As a result, the overwhelming majority of miners utilize specialized mining hardware in the form of cards. These are essentially inserted into the computer in the same way as graphics cards are. You may buy mining gear from well-known manufacturers such as Cointerra, Butterfly Labs, and Bitcoin Ultra, to mention just a few of the available options. Be prepared to fork up some cash, though, since the hardware required for Bitcoin mining may range in price from a few hundred dollars to tens of thousands of dollars. However, if you have the budget for it, it could be worth it to purchase the most expensive one available. The more expensive the machine is, the greater the number of tasks it is able to perform in a given amount of time.

2.A digital currency wallet

You are already familiar with what a wallet is and the reasons why you will require one. The fact that wallets that carry digital money may be typically categorised as either online or local is something that you probably aren't aware of just yet. During the last conversation about exchanges, online wallets were brought up.

Veteran miners typically choose using a local wallet because the data in question is hosted on the internet and is not guaranteed to be 100% safe. The requirement to validate the entirety of the blockchain is the only thing that may dissuade someone from holding their own local wallet. Indeed, this requires investigating each and every Bitcoin transaction that has ever taken place. The completion of this task will take around one day.

You have the option of purchasing from well-known brands such as Armory, BitcoinQT, and Multibit if you aren't concerned with being about one hundred dollars poorer after making the purchase and the thought of having a local wallet appeals to you. It's interesting to note that the last one doesn't need the complete blockchain to be verified.

A word of caution: in contrast to a real wallet, which might save your identity information, so-called virtual wallets do not do so; all that they have is a specific wallet address. If you ever find yourself in a position in the future where you possess a local wallet, ensure that you keep a close check on it at all times. If you misplace your wallet, you will not be able to access any of the bitcoin units that you have mined.

3.One or more Pools

You will also need a pool, but not the sort that has a diving board attached to it. A mining pool is simply a mechanism to gather a group of miners, typically a very big one, who agree to share resources and divide rewards in the event that the proverbial gold is discovered. Your neighborhood wallet can be linked to a larger one.

It would be smart to become a member of a pool. This is particularly relevant in modern times, as the process of obtaining fresh cryptocurrency units for prominent cryptocurrencies like bitcoins is becoming increasingly competitive.
Keep in mind, however, that the fees charged by established mining pools are often somewhere in the range of two percent of what you may expect to make. Additionally, in order to monitor an individual's contributions to a pool, a subaccount that is referred to as a worker has to be established.

Its goal is to guarantee that the individual who made the greatest contribution would also receive the greatest reward for their efforts.

HOW TO JOIN WEBSITES THAT OFFER FREE TRANSFERS

As the use of cryptocurrencies continues to grow, more and more people want to become involved. Joining one of these free transfer platforms is necessary in order to use these currencies. Because there are no transaction fees that are assessed against users, the transfers do not cost anything. There are steps that need to be taken in order to join these sites before you can begin using them.

Those who are interested in cryptocurrencies ought to pick at least one of them to invest in. This is due to the fact that there are more than 15 cryptocurrencies in circulation around the world. This will rely on how easily consumers can enter the market. Restrictions might also serve as a useful way to direct your decision. Those who have been subjected to such severe limitations ought to be avoided.

If it is Namecoin, then they have the option to register for it. In order to sign up, users are required to set up accounts. The wallet is the most crucial thing. When considering whether or not to utilize cryptocurrencies, this is the factor that is most important to consider. The process of creating a wallet could take around ten minutes. On the other hand, there are some that could take even a whole day. It is dependent on the choice that people make.

The following step is to begin converting some of your money into cryptocurrencies. For them to begin trading, their wallets require an initial deposit of some kind. Cryptocurrencies are going to be needed for activities like providing services.

Access to the internet is required before they can begin mining and transmitting currency. Personal computers, on the other hand, need to have impeccable credentials. A productive workday is guaranteed by having high-quality software and hardware.

The next important step is to put in a lot of effort to convince individuals to invest in cryptocurrency. Some people will provide a monetary value for the task that has already been completed.

Mining cryptocurrencies requires some technical know-how and expertise. They demand mental acuity as well as adaptability. This is the hallmark of successful mining. Taking precautions about one's safety is of the utmost importance. There will be certain websites that do not have improved security, which may result in lost cryptocurrencies. Passwords are necessary for men to set up, and it is recommended that they be changed on a frequent basis.

The Characteristics Of Cryptocurrency And Its Use.

Bitcoins and alternative cryptocurrencies have almost the same set of functional and transactional properties, but they cannot be defined by a specific rule set or protocol. This is because the properties cannot be codified. The following is a list of the most often seen characteristics of cryptocurrencies:

Properties relating to transactions (Technical):

Transactions in cryptocurrencies are instantaneous and take place all over the world, but the confirmation of a transaction request often takes only a few minutes at most.

Protected and safe The blockchain technology is incredibly difficult to hack due to the use of tough encryption and a sophisticated mathematical riddle. This is because the blockchain technology uses public key cryptography, which locks all of the cryptocurrencies. The only people who are able to conduct transactions using crypto currencies are the owners of those coins who also possess the private key.

detached from the everyday world
Because cryptocurrencies are entirely digital, there is no physical representation of them anywhere in the world; unlike traditional currencies, you cannot see or touch a cryptocurrency coin in the same way. Each and every transaction as well as the management of the accounts are handled digitally. The word and numeric combinations that make up the coin wallet's digital address each take up 30 of the wallet's total character count. Although it is feasible to analyze the flow of the transaction, it is not possible to relate such analysis to the identity of the sender or recipient in the actual world.

Unchangeable in every way
When a transaction request is confirmed, the transaction becomes permanent, and there is no way to reverse it. This means that when you send cryptocurrency to someone, it is gone forever regardless of whom you send it to. For example, if you enter the wrong address or send it to a scammer by mistake, or if the coin is stolen from your system,

there is nothing that can be done to retrieve it.

Properties pertaining to one's finances (Functional):

a restricted availability of the currency

The 'proof of work concept' the hash algorithm and the blockchain technology have its respective schedule written in such a way that there is quite a bit of restriction in generating cryptocurrencies which ultimately helps in controlling the coin generation. E.g., As per the source code of the bitcoin network, only 21 million Bitcoins can be generated, and once the figure is achieved, it is impossible to generate any more coins. The scarcity of the coin increases its demand thereby mounting its price value.

Only owners (bearers) have access to it.

These digital currencies are similar to gold as they have their own representation, which is why they are referred as 'digital gold' – they represent themselves. One cannot borrow digital currency like fiat money, and therefore they can't be represented as 'debts' like your fiat currency representation in bank accounts.

Tether is what's known as a stablecoin. Because the market as a whole continues to experience such tremendous volatility, it is impossible to have a cryptocurrency that can be described as stable today. Tether provides just what you need if you want to enter the world of cryptocurrencies but keep the value of your dollar intact. This is the case for everybody who wants to do so. When you use it, you get the advantages of both cryptographic and traditional currencies in one convenient package. Your money will be converted into digital currency, and its value will be pegged to that of traditional currencies such as the US dollar, the euro, and the yuan. By making use of it, you can ensure the continued safety of the money you've worked so hard to achieve. You also have a lower probability of losing money. It was established in 2014 with the intention of transforming fiat cash into a digital form that could be utilized throughout the entirety of the blockchain revolution. According to its official website, tether.to, it is "the first blockchain-enabled platform to facilitate the digital use of traditional currencies (a familiar, stable accounting unit)." Tether is credited with democratizing the process of conducting cross-border transactions using blockchain technology. Tether is constructed on the Bitcoin blockchain, which is the longest and oldest blockchain that has ever existed. This gives it a significant advantage over other blockchains. It is now also possible to utilize it on the Ethereum blockchain in the form of smart contracts or decentralized applications (dapps). Because it utilizes USDT, CNHT, and EURT as its base currencies, the exchanges use the letter 'T' to symbolize it, and it is labeled as each of these three fiat currencies. The ability to use traditional currencies within the blockchain ecosystem is a unique feature that it provides. Tether is derived from the definition of the term, which refers to a chain or a rope to which animals can be tethered to restrict their mobility. This is where the company got its name from. The consistent swings in value experienced by the bitcoin market are the type of volatility that Tether intends to counteract. Your comfort level with taking risks is an important question for each potential cryptocurrency investor to ask themselves. How much of a loss in value or money are you able to stomach?

We are now living in a period where, if we invest in cryptocurrencies, we are likely to hear a lot of "I told you so" refrains from the people around us. Even if it is gaining popularity, the ecosystem of cryptocurrencies is still in its infancy stage. In addition to this, it is rather difficult to comprehend for most individuals. However, we frequently forget that in order to buy a car or a dishwasher, we do not always need to have a complete understanding of how their internal workings operate. If you don't understand how blockchains function or how currencies are mined, it's not the end of the world; but, it will make things easier for you if you do. You are not required to do so. as long as you have an understanding of the ideology behind the currency or the driving force behind it. The purpose it intends to serve. There are cellphones everywhere you look these days. But let's not sugarcoat things here. There are still many people in the globe who are unfamiliar with how to get the most of the many applications of the smartphone. Do virtual currencies have the capacity to become widely used in every sector of the economy? This is a question that we will need to ask ourselves in due time if it turns out that cryptocurrencies are the future of money, as the majority of cryptocurrencies have declared themselves to be.

The straightforward response to the question "why use Tether" is that people do so because it is reliable. It is linked or connected to the fiat currencies that are used in the actual world. You may give the world of cryptocurrencies a try, and if you find that it is not for you, you can always withdraw your digital money without suffering any kind of loss. There are no great plans in place to construct a future digital economy that is decentralized or to tackle the problems that plague the planet. Instead of doing that, you may trade in your dollars for tethers and carry out all of these transactions on websites that support tether transactions. The cryptography prompts the question, "What do you lose in the process?" as a natural follow-up. Because of this, Tether is a reliable platform on which to start your exploration of the cryptocurrency world. The advantage of utilizing it is that you will not unexpectedly find yourself on unfamiliar territory. It is a decentralized form of value exchange that

makes use of the blockchain mechanism of

peer-to-peer transactions.

The reserve ratio of a Tether token held in relation to a fiat currency is kept constant at one to one by Tether. The amount of money that is believed to be held by banks and other centralized organizations throughout the world is currently estimated to be around 250 trillion dollars. Imagine for a moment that all of that could be transferred to the more stable and profitable realm of digital money. You do not need to make investments in other blockchains since it operates on the blockchain that Bitcoin has already developed because it is already in existence. It operates in the same manner that Bitcoin does. You are free to purchase, sell, or put a reservation in for an unlimited number of Tethers. Its pegging makes it simpler to adopt for non-technical users who are confused by all of the jargon that is associated with the cryptocurrency sector. The goal is straightforward: to facilitate more widespread use of digital currencies in preparation for future innovation and expansion.

Wallets and exchangers are not a very dependable option in the modern day. To offer a remedy, Tether suggests a 'Proof of Reserves'. It is an innovative technique that establishes that the amount of value that is circulating in Tethers is backed by an equivalent quantity of fiat money that is kept in reserves. Specifically, this approach proves that. Each Tether that is in circulation corresponds to one US Dollar that is either in circulation or being kept in reserve.

As of right now, the most prominent issuer of stablecoins is Tether. The value of its market capitalization is currently at around 58 billion dollars. As of right now, this places it as the third most valuable cryptocurrency out of the top ten list. Very recently, it made the announcement that it will be accessible on Avalanche, which is a future platform that will support decentralized finance and smart contracts. Even though Avalanche will only be one year old in 2021, it has already demonstrated very encouraging development. Paolo Ardoino is the Chief Technical Officer of Tether, and he made the assertion that the cheap transaction costs offered by Avalanche will encourage the transfer of users from fiat currencies to cryptocurrency. In a market that is quite volatile, it is important to keep in mind that Tether provides stability and protection for the money you have.

Do You Require The Services Of A Trading Broker?

It's possible that opening an account with a trading broker is no longer required if all you want to do is invest in bitcoin or another cryptocurrency that's already established. This is due to the fact that certain cryptocurrency wallets, such as Coinbase, will provide you the ability to purchase and sell certain cryptocurrencies directly from your wallet. This is an excellent option, especially if your only goal is to create an investment for the long term. However, if you want to actively trade cryptocurrencies or if you are looking for a site where you can quickly purchase and sell cryptocurrencies, including lesser-known altcoins, you will need to establish an account with a cryptocurrency trading broker. If you do not have such an account, you will not be able to actively trade cryptocurrencies. When working with a broker, opening a trading account is a quick and painless process. In most cases, the procedure may be finished in significantly less than five minutes.

You may discover a large number of cryptocurrency brokers who provide services that are practically identical to one another by executing a simple search on the internet. It is critical for you to ensure that the trading broker you choose is reputable and genuine if you plan to engage in investing or trading. There are specific criteria that you need to take into consideration while selecting a broker to trade cryptocurrencies, including the following:

Commentary on...

Checking out the most recent evaluations that other investors have left for your selected trading broker is the first step you ought to do before making any kind of financial deposit or buying bitcoin from that broker. To do this, all you need to do is open up your browser of choice, type in the name of the broker, and then follow it up with the term "reviews." For instance, if you are interested in learning what others have to say about the trading broker known as Bitfinex, all you need to do is perform a search using the following query: bitfinex reviews. After that, the search engine will display relevant pages to you. You should read the reviews that have been offered to the broker and pay attention to both the positive and negative things that others have stated about the broker that you have selected. In addition to this, you need to check the dates to see when the most recent reviews were made. It is important to keep in mind, once more, that prior to making any kind of deposit or spending any kind of real money, you should make it a point to read and carefully consider the evaluations that have been offered to the broker.

The platform for trading

You will be given access to a trading platform by your broker so that you may engage in cryptocurrency trading and investment activities. The trading platform that your broker offers you should, as a general rule, be straightforward and uncomplicated to use. After all, it is the responsibility of your broker to simplify the trading process for you, and not the other way around. You should not expect your broker to do the opposite. Even if it is only of minor importance, having a trading platform that is properly built is still helpful. This is to assist in getting you in the frame of mind necessary for trading successfully.

Additionally, the interface of the platform need to be simple to use. It should not be difficult for you to navigate the platform, particularly the most crucial components of it. Last but not least, your trading broker should give you with useful tools that you can use to come up with a trading choice, such as graphs and charts that indicate the price fluctuations of the various cryptocurrencies that are currently on the market. These resources should be available to you at all times.

Version optimized for mobile use.

Accessing the internet through your mobile phone is currently the method of choice since it is both more handy and quicker. Trading platforms for cryptocurrencies are aware of this fact. Because of this, the brokerage firm that you work with should also provide you a mobile version of the trading platform they use. The mobile version need to be intuitive to use and should provide access to all of the functions that are required. Using the mobile version, you should have no trouble managing your account or buying and selling cryptocurrencies. Additionally, you should be able to do so with ease. Even if it might not have all of the capabilities that are available in the desktop version of the trading platform, it is still required to have all of the features that are necessary and crucial for the platform. It is not necessary for you to be concerned about this matter because all reputable trading brokers will provide you access to an expert mobile version of the platform that is stocked with everything you want in order to invest in and trade cryptocurrencies.

Customer service that is actively engaged

It is of the utmost importance for you, as a cryptocurrency investor or trader, to collaborate with a broker that possesses both an active and responsive customer care staff. In your professional life, you will find this to be the case. In the normal course of events, a broker will provide you an email address via which you may communicate with the support staff. It is also possible that it has a specific page on its website where you may communicate with the customer care team by sending a message. It is even possible that it will provide a live on-page function, in addition to providing a number that you may contact. Note the several channels via which you may get in touch with the customer support team. This will most certainly come in helpful in the event that you have any inquiries or if you ever run into any technical issues.

It is also recommended that you evaluate the level of quality and responsiveness provided by the customer care personnel. Sending an inquiry is a useful method for accomplishing this goal. You are free to ask any pertinent question that comes to mind. The next step for you to do is to examine how quickly and expertly the customer service personnel handles and resolves your query. You should ideally receive a response from your trading broker within twenty-four hours at the most.

The conditions for deposits and withdrawals

Check your broker's minimum and maximum deposit and withdrawal limits, as well as any other limitations that may apply. This information is often located on the page that pertains to banking. Do not be afraid to get in touch with the customer support team if you are unable to discover what you are looking for. In addition to this, you should be wary of any withdrawal requirements that may be imposed by your broker. In most cases, making a deposit is relatively simple, but when you request a withdrawal, there is a possibility that you may run into some difficulties. This is especially true if this is your first time requesting a withdrawal. Before processing a withdrawal request, it is not unusual for trading brokers to request specific identifying papers from their customers, such as a scanned copy of their legitimate government-issued identification and proof of invoicing. Before you even consider making a deposit, check to see that you have all of these documents on hand and in your possession. If you do not comply, there is a possibility that you may be unable to withdraw all of the money that is currently in your account. This includes any gains that you may have made. Also, find out how long it will take your broker to process a withdrawal request and get that information. If everything goes according to plan, you should be able to get the requested withdrawal in your bitcoin wallet within twenty-four hours, providing that you have also satisfied with any documentation requirements that your broker may have.

coins and tokens available on the market for trading

Your trading broker ought to provide you with access to a comprehensive range of cryptocurrencies that are available for trading or investment on their platform. The more digital currencies that are made available to you by your broker, the more variety of options you will have. It is to your advantage if your broker provides access to new altcoins because of the significant potential profits associated with trading in these cryptocurrencies.

Trading on the margin

There are brokers out there that could give you permission to trade on margin. When you engage in margin trading, you are essentially borrowing cryptocurrency from your broker. This can be useful, especially when you are just getting started and have a limited amount of cash. It's possible that a broker may let you use up to 70 percent of your invested cash for margin trading. However, exercise extreme caution while trading on margin. Because you will be borrowing cryptocurrency from your broker, you will be required to pay your broker interest on the borrowed cryptocurrency. After all, no broker worth their salt would ever give you free cryptocurrency for no reason at all. There is never a situation without a catch. It is strongly recommended that you do not engage in trading on margin if you are just starting out in the market. Just use the money that you already have invested, and then you won't have to worry about having to pay any interest on it. Trading on margin exposes one to the possibility of incurring losses over time.

The Market's Mood

Traders have been taking advantage of the markets for as long as the markets have existed, and they have been using the word "market sentiment" ever since. This term is often used to characterize the mood of the general public in relation to an asset or market. One of the most typical ways that it is defined is as a short-term trend, which basically just means that the general public has an opinion on the path that an asset and its value is taking at any particular point in time.

When it comes to any particular asset at any particular time, there will always be some form of market mood associated with it. It is crucial to become familiar with these various kinds of market sentiment in order to have a better understanding of how they can be used and what they imply in order to figure out the best way to trade. Market sentiment may be a vital factor to consider when attempting to figure out the best way to trade.

Why Is It So Important to Track Market Sentiment?

To begin, it is essential to have an understanding of the connection that exists between the emotion of the market and the real assets that comprise a particular market. When you look at a market and watch the assets trading in different ways, you will typically find that those assets that are more impacted by the public mood tend to be more volatile than other assets. This is because public sentiment tends to be a leading indicator of market volatility.

The reason for this is that more individuals are trading these assets than are trading other assets, and any form of movement in public opinion will often effect them more adversely than it does other assets. It also implies that if you want to be successful as a trader, it is essential to pay attention to these movements regardless of what you are trading in order to maximize your chances of being successful.

Which Categories of Emotion Are There to Choose From?

There are a number distinct types of market mood, but the overall bullishness (reflecting positive news) and bearishness (reflecting negative news) are the two that have the greatest weight in the market. The first action is more commonly referred to as purchasing, whereas the second action is more commonly known as selling. Again, these are only two broad forms that may be seen within virtually every market at any given moment; but, depending on a variety of conditions, one of these forms is going to be more obvious than the other.

It is also essential to keep in mind that there are no genuine laws governing the manner in which these things should behave in relation to markets. They are really simply a general rule of thumb that will surely apply most of the time but can be modified by other influences just like anything else. Although they will definitely apply most of the time, they will definitely not apply all of the time. The fact that market mood is one of the few aspects that can be manipulated, at least in principle, makes it extremely relevant to consider while engaging in financial trading.

Adapting Your Trading to the Market's Mood

You should always trade with the sentiment in a market, at least to some extent, according to the general consensus. If there is more purchasing going on than selling going on (bullish), you want to make sure that you are on the other side of those sell deals so that you may profit from the price increase. If there are more people selling than purchasing (bearish), you should make every effort to trade in a way that goes against the mood as much as possible during these periods of time. This is due to the fact that it is difficult to earn money while trading against the emotion of the market since doing so involves entering a transaction at the worst possible time, which makes it difficult to make money. Although it is possible to accomplish, it is not encouraged due to the fact that there are far greater prospects to be found in other parts of the market.

How do you evaluate someone's state of mind?

You may do a few things to assist obtain a sense of how much of a market is being driven by sentiment at any one time, even if it can be tough to figure out how much of a market is being driven by sentiment at any particular time. Taking a look at the price activity and attempting to formulate a hypothesis on the factors that may affect the price is the simplest approach. This is an excellent place to start, but if you want to make an accurate assessment, you will eventually need to take into consideration a greater number of criteria.

You simply need to look at two factors in order to understand how people feel about the market: the bid-ask spread and the volatility. You may get an indication of how much money is being put into the market (through sales), as well as how much money is flowing out (through purchases), by looking at the bid/ask spread for an asset. When trade shifts from one side of the spread to the other, it is typically a very strong indicator that sentiment has shifted. This may happen when the trade moves from one side of the spread to the other.

Volatility can also provide you some indicator regarding sentiment, but it is not as easy to pinpoint as the bid/ask spread is. Volatility can be measured by the standard deviation of prices. The reason for this is simply that when you look at the price chart, which has a more direct link to actual money flows, it is not as linear as you might expect it to be. To put it simply, there will be a lot of volatility in the market if there are many trades in the direction of buying an asset but none in the direction of selling the item. This is the best possible circumstance to be in since it indicates that other traders have recognized the volatile market conditions and wish to capitalize on them.

When trying to determine how sentiment could be impacting an asset, it is always vital to keep these two criteria in mind. However, depending on the sort of information you're looking for, you might also test a number of other things. These are the following:

You will have a better understanding of the amount of money that is being traded in an asset by looking at the volume data, which include open interest and volume levels. When it comes to futures and options, this is of utmost significance since you will frequently observe greater trading activity in these markets due to the fact that they may be subject to less regulation than other markets. There is a lot of buying pressure

165

because there has been an increase in volume, which indicates that other traders are taking advantage of the price changes. (If you are interested in a certain type of option or futures contract, you should keep this fact in mind.)

When it comes to commodity futures markets, commodity prices should be monitored since they typically offer a highly accurate barometer of public mood. This is especially true when it comes to energy commodities like oil and natural gas. Especially when it comes to energy commodities like oil and natural gas. This is not the case with stocks, which more often than not have a direct link with the success of companies rather than with the feelings of the broader population. Just make sure that you keep an eye on the markets for commodities that are regularly traded because the price action is frequently influenced by shifts in public perception.

Indicators of the economy should also be observed, particularly in relation to markets that are driven by news, such as currency pairings or bonds that are directly linked to an economy or country. There is a good chance that they will have an impact on other assets as well, although they will often begin in one of these markets and then spread to others via movement speculation and transfer. If you know how to look at the market and what causes may impact market sentiment in a timely manner, it is not hard to find out how market sentiment is affecting an asset. In general, it is quite straightforward to figure out how market sentiment is affecting an asset. When it comes to trading, it is essential to keep in mind that there are no ironclad laws governing market emotions.

This indicates that there will always be certain opportunities that you will need to make the most of as well. When it comes to long or short trades, it is important to keep in mind that not all assets will act in accordance with the same patterns at any given moment. As a result, it is imperative that you be familiar with these patterns.

The fact that markets might behave in a variety of ways, depending on a variety of circumstances with which you are unaware, is one of the things that makes trading in markets so intriguing. One of the never-ending problems that helps make trading such a wonderful activity is the fact that you can never truly predict how the market will behave until it actually does so. In the next chapters, we will go through some of the several approaches you may use to capitalize on the mood of the market. It is not necessary for you to immediately enter a transaction simply because the price of an asset is moving in either the up or down direction. You want to make sure that you enter the market at the optimal moment and price so that you don't end up with a lost transaction or a drawdown.

www.ingramcontent.com/pod-product-compliance
Lightning Source LLC
Chambersburg PA
CBHW071234210326
41597CB00016B/2055